BOBBY & MANDEE'S

Good Touch Bad Touch

Hey, parents! Read this book with your kids!

Not all touches are good, so be aware!

CHILDREN'S SAFETY BOOK

Robert Kahn

with illustrations by Lynda Farrington Wilson

Bobby & Mandee's Good Touch Bad Touch

All marketing and publishing rights guaranteed to and reserved by:

FUTURE HORIZONS INC.

817·277·0727 | Fax: 817·277·2270
www.FHautism.com | info@FHautism.com

ISBN: 9781949177954

DEDICATION

I wish to thank my family and friends for all of their support with this book.

Hello again, I am Bobby and you remember my sister, Mandee. Usually, we are keeping you safe from strangers. However, this book is different: this danger may not come from a stranger, but usually happens with someone you know well.

Today we are going to talk about **GOOD TOUCHES**, and **BAD TOUCHES**.

Whether it is a stranger, or someone you know well, the rules to be safe are always the same:

SAY NO! RUN AWAY!
AND FIND A GROWN-UP FRIEND TO TELL!

Now let's start out by explaining
GOOD TOUCHES.

GOOD TOUCHES are the following:
Hugs, kisses, a pat on the shoulder, a pat on the back,
a pat on the head, a hand shake, or a "HIGH 5."
These are all **GOOD TOUCHES**.

Now let's discuss **BAD TOUCHES**.
A BAD TOUCH makes you feel creepy inside
your body. A **BAD TOUCH** can also hurt you.

Here are some **BAD TOUCHES**:
A hit, slap, punch, kick, bite, hard pinch, shove,
grabbing, tugging, scratching, tripping,
and choking.

You always have the right to be safe and if any of these things happens to you, no matter who is doing it, *SAY NO! RUN AWAY! AND FIND A GROWN-UP FRIEND TO TELL!*

If the first grown-up you tell doesn't believe you, don't stop telling what is happening to you.
Tell, until someone believes you!

There are adults you can always tell if a **BAD TOUCH** is happening to you. They are: Your teacher, counselor, principal, school nurse, school secretary, your doctor, or a police person.

Now there is one more **BAD TOUCH** which we have to discuss. This is touching your body's private areas.

The reason they are called **"PRIVATES"**
is because they belong only to you.

Your bathing suit covers the area that is
PRIVATE only to you.

A doctor may have to examine your private areas when you are getting a physical exam to make sure you are healthy.

If you ever get hurt, mom or dad may have to help you bathe. But otherwise, no one should be touching your privates.

If this is happening to you, or one of your friends, you need to tell a trusted adult. *This isn't your fault! The one touching you is doing bad things!*

The person touching you may be someone who lives with you, or a close friend of the family.

If someone is touching you in a way that makes you feel uncomfortable, **they will also tell you things which are not true.**

They may say something like, "If you tell, your mother won't love you anymore!" Or, "You and I have a big secret to keep!"

"If you tell, I'll know" and "People will be mad at you!" Another one is, "If you tell, I'll hurt your dog!"

Don't believe anything they might tell you!
These are "BAD TRICKS" so that you won't tell.

The only reason they are saying these things is so
that they won't get in trouble. Remember, you haven't
done anything wrong! *They are the ones who will be
in trouble, NOT YOU!*

You and your friends have the right to be safe.
You are not being safe if someone is touching
you in a way that is wrong or that makes you
feel uncomfortable.

If you, or one of your friends, are being
touched or hurt in any way,

SAY NO! RUN AWAY!
AND FIND A GROWN-UP FRIEND TO TELL!

Mandee and I hope you have learned about **GOOD TOUCHES** and **BAD TOUCHES** by reading our book.

Bobby and Mandee's Touch Test

1. Name some "GOOD TOUCHES." (answer on page 3)

   _____

   _____

2. Name some "BAD TOUCHES." (answer on page 4)

   _____

   _____

3. If someone touches you in a bad way, what should you do?
   (answer on page 5-6)

   _____

   _____

4. Why are they called "PRIVATES"? (answer on page 8)

   _____

   _____

5. A bathing suit covers what? (answer on page 9)

   _____

   _____

6. If someone touches your privates, what should you do? (answer on page 11)

   _____

   _____

7. Who are trusted adults you can talk to if someone gives you a BAD TOUCH? (answer on page 6)

   _____

   _____

8. Is it your fault if someone touches your privates? (answer on page 11)

_____

_____

9. What should you do if someone touches your privates and says, "We have a big secret to keep. People won't like us any-more if they find out, so let's not tell anyone." (answer on page 14)

_____

_____

10. Why are they telling you a story like that? (answer on page 15)

_____

_____

11. All children have the right to be _____. (answer on page 15)

12. If a person does this to you, do you think they are only doing it to you and not other children? (This is a thought question for the child)

_____

_____

Secrets and Surprises— There's a Big Difference!

On page 13, we talked about how adults may ask you to keep a secret, and that is probably not a good thing. But an adult may ask you to keep some information for a surprise. Do you know the difference between a secret and a surprise?

A **SURPRISE** is something that you WILL tell someone soon, and it should be a good surprise. Like a birthday present or a surprise party. You are keeping information from someone for a GOOD reason and for a short time, expecting that they will be happy when they know it.

A **SECRET** is something that someone asks you NEVER to tell anyone. If an adult asks you to keep a surprise for a while, that is probably okay. But if an adult asks you to keep a SECRET, they may be trying to hide something bad they did. You should tell someone you trust.

Can you list some surprises? Things that are okay to keep for a short time?

_____

_____

_____

_____

_____

_____

_____

_____

_____

_____

911 Tips for Parents

1. Teach your children how to dial 911. A call to 911 should always be a call for help. You can call 911 from the lock screen of anyone's cell phone. On the passcode screen, just tap **Emergency**.

Do your children know when to call 911?

- If there is someone injured or sick.
- If there is smoke or flames in the house.
- If they are home alone and someone is trying to get in.
- If a stranger follows them home from school.
- If they see a car accident.
- If they observe someone being hurt by another person.
- If during a storm, they see a power pole or another object struck by lightning.

Do your children know when NOT to call 911?

- Never call 911 as a joke!
- Never call 911 just for information.
- Never call 911 just to see if it works!

2. Be sure to stress the following two points with your child:

- NEVER get into a car with someone unless your parents know you're going with that person.
- ALWAYS tell your parents where you're going.

Other Important Information:

Children need to know their address, phone number, and the type of emergency help they need.

- Address_____
- Phone _____
- Police _____
- Fire _____
- Medical _____

My List of Safe Grown-Ups to Call

NAME	PHONE NUMBER
_____	_____
_____	_____
_____	_____
_____	_____
_____	_____
_____	_____
_____	_____
_____	_____
_____	_____

Color Us!

Look for more of our books about being **SAFE**.

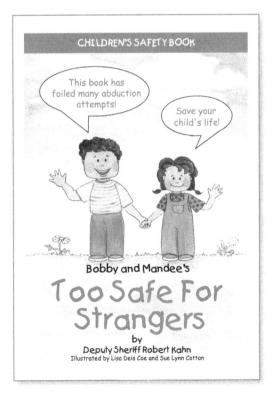